MASTER YOUR PROFESSIONAL GOALS WITH NUMEROLOGY

Embrace Opportunities, Navigate Life's Challenges, Craft Your Desired Career, and Transform Goals into Reality Via Personalized Numerological Approach

SOORAJ ACHAR

WWW.SOORAJ-ACHAR.COM

YOUR FREE GIFT !!

A s a token of my thanks for taking out time to read my book, I would like to offer you a **Free-Gift**:

Scan Below **QR Code** to Download your **Free eBook PDF**.

Learn 395+ Surprising Psychology Words That Will Change The Way You Think - in the Next 30 Days!

You can also grab your **FREE GIFT** by typing in the below URL: **https://gift.sooraj-achar.com/**

ABOUT AUTHOR

Sooraj Achar, the Accomplished Author of "**Master Your PROFESSIONAL GOALS With Numerology**" - A Sensational **#1 Bestseller Across the Globe**

Dive into the world of **Sooraj Achar**, a prodigious author hailing from Bangalore, India, whose exceptional journey is as intriguing as the profound concepts explored in his works. With "The Fear of Death," Sooraj has transcended borders, achieving the coveted status of **#1 Bestseller** in the United States, the United Kingdom, Canada, India, and Australia.

A Remarkable Beginnings:

Sooraj Achar's extraordinary odyssey commenced in the vibrant city of Bangalore, India. As a young dreamer, his fascination with mathematics sparked an early connection with the enigmatic world of numbers. This infatuation, initially drawn from captivating numerological stories, sowed the seeds for a lifetime dedicated to the exploration of **Numerical Mysteries**.

A Multifaceted Expert:

Today, **Sooraj Achar** stands as not just an accomplished Software Engineer but also a passionate connoisseur of **numerology** and the ancient science of **Feng-Shui (Vastu)**. His multifaceted persona extends to **coaching and consulting**, where he delves into the profound questions of Health, Relationships, Careers, and Money (HRCM). Sooraj is a certified **Ho'oponopono & EFT Healer and NLP Practitioner**, renowned for his transformative abilities in bringing about balance, harmony, and fulfillment in the lives of countless individuals.

A Seeker of Wisdom:

Sooraj's relentless quest for knowledge has led him to the intricate realms of human psychology and behavior. His dedication to understanding the human psyche and optimizing life's potential is unwavering. As a perpetual learner, he embodies the principles of optimal living and shares his wisdom to empower others to lead resourceful lives.

A Believer in Unlimited Potential:

Above all, **Sooraj Achar** is a firm believer in the limitless potential residing within each individual. He ardently champions the idea that every person possesses the capacity to achieve far beyond their self-imposed limits. Through his words and wisdom, he inspires others to unlock their hidden potential and lead lives of purpose and abundance.

For more life-altering insights, delve into Sooraj Achar's remarkable catalog of books. Visit www.sooraj-achar.com and embark on a journey of self-discovery and transformation.

Stay Connected:

Explore the latest updates, thought-provoking content, and inspiring messages from Sooraj Achar by connecting with him through our social media channels. Join us in the pursuit of a fulfilling and harmonious life.

https://amzn.to/3CgQHF9

https://medium.com/@soorajachar99

https://bit.ly/3M7gIu2

instagram.com/psychology_of_numberz/

https://bit.ly/3dO6aDh

https://bit.ly/3LXBTyz

https://bit.ly/3E9vKxc

ACKNOWLEDGMENT

How does a person say "**Thank You**" when there are so many people to thank?

Obviously, this book is a big thank you to my father **G Sathyanarayan Achar,** who is a powerful role model, and my mother **G Pramila,** who taught me love and kindness.

I extend my heartfelt appreciation to my sister, **Shruthi S**, brother-in-law, **Saravana P**, and adorable niece, **Naveeksha S**, who have played pivotal roles in making this book a reality. Their presence makes my life complete.

A special acknowledgment is reserved for my mentor, **Mr. Arvind Sood**, whose guidance led me to become a **Numerology and Vaastu Coach and Consultant**. I am privileged to have received permission to use the term "Driver-Conductor," a creation of Mr. Arvind Sood.

I owe thanks to **Mr. Som Bathla**, an **Amazon #1 Bestselling** author, for his mentorship, motivation, and guidance in the realms of **Writing, Self-Publishing, and Launching Books**. His support has been instrumental in initiating my journey as an Authorpreneur.

Finally, heartfelt gratitude to my dedicated team – **Avesh Ansari**, **Akshay Bhat**, and **Md. Bilal** – for their unwavering support and contributions.

DEDICATION

This Book is Dedicated to My Grandparents,

R. Gangadhar & G. Vishalakshamma

And, My Dear Brother **Arvind Achar.**

CONTENTS

How This Book Can Work Miracles in Your Life? XV

Chapter Highlights: Top 5 Takeaways & Insights XXIV

IMPORTANT! - Before You Proceed XL

1. Find Your Suitable Profession - Job Or Business? 1

2. Detect Your Foreign Opportunities & Abroad Settlement 4

3. Professions As Per The Lines in Your Birth Chart 12

4. Find Your Lucky & Unlucky Colors 16

5. Is Your Child Weak in Studies? 24

6. How to Detect Education Sector?   27

7. Profession of Anti & Opposite D-C   34
   Combination

8. Trying Hard To Get a Government Job?   39

9. Who Can Be A Coach And A Player?   42

10. Mobile Numerology   46

11. Design Your Visiting/Business Card   50

12. Top-5 Case Studies   52

Conclusion   64

May I Ask You For A Small Favor?   66

Preview of My Best Selling Books   69

Testimonials   86

Author Profile   92

Disclaimer   95

HOW THIS BOOK CAN WORK MIRACLES IN YOUR LIFE?

In the vast tapestry of life, where every thread is woven with experiences, choices, and aspirations, the quest for professional success stands as a prominent motif. "Master Your PROFESSIONAL GOALS With Numerology" is not just a book; it is a transformative guide that can work miracles in your life, illuminating the path to success and fulfillment.

Understanding the Power of Numerology

At its core, numerology is more than a mystical art; it is a language that deciphers the numerical codes embedded in our existence. This book serves as your interpreter, unraveling the secrets that numbers hold about your professional journey. Each digit, each calculation, becomes a compass guiding you through the labyrinth of choices, opportunities, and challenges.

Embracing Opportunities

The book is your portal to a realm where opportunities are not left to chance but are strategically embraced. By delving into the depths of your numerological profile, you gain insights into the opportunities that align with your inherent strengths and propensities. It's not just about chance encounters; it's about creating a landscape where opportunities flourish and success becomes a natural progression.

Navigating Life's Challenges

Challenges are not roadblocks but stepping stones in the journey toward your professional goals. This book equips you with the wisdom to navigate challenges with resilience and strategic acumen. Your numerological blueprint becomes a guide, providing you with a nuanced understanding of how to turn obstacles into opportunities and transform setbacks into catalysts for growth.

Crafting Your Desired Career

Your career is not a happenstance occurrence; it is a creation, a masterpiece that you sculpt with intention and precision. "Master Your PROFESSIONAL GOALS With Numerology" empowers you to craft your desired career with a personalized approach. By aligning your choices with the vibrational frequencies of your numerological profile, you become the architect of a career that resonates with your true self.

Transforming Goals into Reality

Goals, once nebulous aspirations, crystallize into tangible realities through the alchemy of numerology. This book provides you with the tools to transform your professional dreams into achievable milestones. It's not just wishful thinking; it's a strategic roadmap where each goal is anchored in the numerical currents that flow through your life.

Personalized Numerological Approach

The magic of this book lies in its personalized approach. It recognizes that each individual is a unique combination of energies, talents, and challenges. Through a detailed exploration of your numerological profile, you receive tailored guidance. It's not a one-size-fits-all solution; it's a bespoke map that unfolds the terrain of your professional destiny.

20 Major Benefits of Reading "Master Your PROFESSIONAL GOALS With Numerology"

1. Personalized Guidance: Receive personalized insights into your professional journey based on your unique numerological profile.

2. Strategic Decision-Making: Learn to make strategic decisions aligned with your numerological blueprint, navigating professional complexities with confidence.

3. Opportunity Alignment: Identify and embrace opportunities that resonate with your inherent strengths and propensities.

4. Career Crafting: Craft your desired career with intention, ensuring alignment with your true self and professional aspirations.

5. Challenges as Stepping Stones: Transform challenges into stepping stones, understanding how obstacles can propel you toward growth and success.

6. Financial Empowerment: Gain a profound understanding of your financial strengths and weaknesses through the numerological lens.

7. Financial Personality Analysis: Receive a personalized analysis of your financial personality, going beyond conventional financial advice.

8. Wealth Mindset Cultivation: Cultivate an abundance mindset that transforms your approach to wealth and prosperity.

9. Hidden Financial Messages: Unveil hidden messages embedded in your financial experiences, conquering hidden obstacles with numerological wisdom.

10. Alignment with Destiny: Align your financial choices with your destiny, creating a harmonious relationship between your numerological profile and financial success.

11. Positive Financial Environment: Leverage lucky numbers and colors to create a positive financial environment that enhances your overall well-being.

12. Informed Investments: Make informed investment decisions considering the numerological implications for long-term success.

13. Career Harmony: Integrate your career path with your numerological harmony, ensuring professional fulfillment and success.

14. Entrepreneurial Guidance: Receive a numerological blueprint to guide your business ventures, increasing the likelihood of success and prosperity.

15. Enhanced Relationship Dynamics: Explore the numerological dynamics of financial relationships, fostering harmony in partnerships and collaborations.

16. Strategic Forecasting: Develop the ability to forecast your financial future with a numerological crystal ball, identifying significant years, months, and days for strategic decisions.

17. Career Alignment with Numerology: Understand how your career is intricately woven into the fabric of your numerological destiny, ensuring a fulfilling professional journey.

18. Goal Transformation: Transform nebulous professional goals into tangible realities through the alchemy of numerology.

19. Enhanced Decision-Making: Experience heightened clarity in decision-making, leveraging numerological insights for professional choices.

20. Holistic Approach to Success: Embrace a holistic approach to success, where every aspect of your professional life is guided by the wisdom of numerology, leading to enduring fulfillment and accomplishment.

Purpose Behind Crafting This Book !!

The impetus behind the creation of this book is rooted in the need to address and provide clarity on questions similar to the ones posed above. My objective has been to elucidate the fundamental truths regarding strengths and weaknesses in a language that is both accessible and straightforward. I firmly believe in the ability to articulate the foundational laws governing life and the mind using ordinary, everyday language.

The language employed in this book mirrors that which is commonly found in your daily newspapers, business offices, homes, and workplaces. My encouragement to you is to delve into the contents of this book and implement the techniques outlined within. In doing so, I am confident that you will harness a miraculous power capable of lifting you from confusion, misery, and failure, guiding you toward your rightful place. This transformative power has the capacity to resolve your difficulties, liberate you from emotional and physical constraints, and set you on the regal path to freedom, happiness, and peace of mind.

The miraculous potential embedded in your date of birth is akin to a healing force, capable of fortifying your weaknesses, restoring vitality, and steering your life journey through the profound principles of Numerology.

CHAPTER HIGHLIGHTS: TOP 5 TAKEAWAYS & INSIGHTS

1. Key Takeaways for the Chapter - Find Your Suitable Profession - Job Or Business?

1. Driver-Centric Career Guidance: Explore career suitability based on your driver number. The chapter provides clear associations between driver numbers (1-9) and their compatibility with business, jobs, or both.

2. Conductor Consideration: Emphasizes the significance of conductor influence in career choices. It's

not just about the driver; a harmonious combination with the conductor is crucial for optimal career decisions.

3. Holistic Decision-Making: Recommends avoiding a myopic focus on the driver or conductor alone. Instead, suggests selecting a career number aligned with both for a comprehensive and balanced approach.

4. Yog and Chart Dynamics: Acknowledges the role of favorable Yog and chart lines in enhancing career prospects. Even if a driver suggests a certain inclination, chart dynamics can open avenues for success in unexpected areas.

5. Nuanced Approach for Specific Drivers: Illustrates a nuanced approach, such as the example of the driver 7, where despite its association with jobs, it can excel in business, particularly in property and real estate, given certain chart conditions.

2. Key Takeaways for the Chapter - Detect Your Foreign Opportunities & Abroad Settlement

1. Numerical Destinies: Discover the impact of your date of birth on your potential for success in a job or business, highlighting the significance of your driver, conductor, and birth chart.

2. Driver Decisions: Choose your career path wisely by aligning it with your driver number, understanding the favorable and unfavorable options for each number from 1 to 9.

3. Complementary Success: Even if your driver number suggests a preference for a job or business, explore the complementary numbers in your chart that could unlock unexpected opportunities.

4. Yogic Influence: Delve into the importance of favorable Yog and lines in your chart, understanding how they can influence your success in business, even if your driver number indicates a preference for a job.

5. International Prospects: Explore the numerology of foreign settlement, evaluate the impact of numbers 5 and 6, and determine the compatibility of your driver and conductor for success in a foreign country or your homeland.

3. Key Takeaways for the Chapter - Professions As Per The Lines In Your Birth Chart

1. Career Symphony: Let numerology guide your career melody, uncovering the professions associated with specific lines or yogas in your birth chart.

2. Thought Plane Professions (4-3-8): Navigate a career in politics, marketing, sales, law, or judiciary, understanding the influence of knowledge, logic, and dedication.

3. Will Plane Versatility (9-5-1): Embrace a diverse range of professions, with a focus on the banking sector and opportunities in agriculture, property, and real estate.

4. Action Plane Success (2-7-6): Thrive in physical activities, excelling in sports like cricket, football, and

hockey, while also exploring avenues in the occult, luxury, fashion, and beauty.

5. Practical Plane Excellence (8-1-6): Flourish in the commercial world, succeeding in business, entrepreneurship, and ventures related to luxury, glamor, hotels, and salons. Explore opportunities in law, judiciary, and politics for a well-rounded career.

6. Raj Yoga Lines: Unleash exponential earning potential with lines like 4-5-6 in businesses such as hotels, restaurants, salons, luxury, glamor, garments, casinos, and liquor.

7. Raj Yoga 2 Opportunities (2-5-8): Explore a destined path in real estate, property, agriculture, or banking and financial sectors, leveraging the strength of numbers 5 and 8 for success.

4. Key Takeaways for the Chapter - Find Your Lucky & Unlucky Colors

1. Decoding Colors: Understand the significance of colors in your life by decoding which ones are friendly and non-friendly based on your numerological profile.

2. Personalized Color Selection: Learn how to choose colors that match your driver and conductor numbers, ensuring harmony and positive energy in your surroundings.

3. Avoiding Non-Friendly Colors: Gain insights into colors to avoid, such as black, and the rationale behind steering clear of them to prevent potential challenges and struggles.

4. Importance of Friendly Colors: Discover the impact of utilizing friendly colors, as they can act as catalysts in enhancing progress and positivity in various aspects of life.

5. Color-Sharing Planets: Navigate through the complexity of planets sharing the same color and learn which numbers take priority in case of conflicts, providing clarity in selecting auspicious colors for personal and environmental choices.

5. Key Takeaways for the Chapter - Is Your Child Weak In Studies?

1. Yoga of Study: Explore the numerological indicators in your child's date of birth to determine if they possess a strong "yoga of study," revealing their potential for academic brilliance.

2. Exceptional Abilities: Identify the exceptional abilities of your child by examining the presence of numbers 3 (Jupiter) and 7 (Ketu) in their date of birth, indicating a combination of knowledge and wisdom.

3. Loshu Grid Analysis: Evaluate the support of the top line (line of 4,9,2) in the Loshu grid, considering its influence on your child's academic prowess.

4. Extraordinary Child: If your child has all five numbers (including 3 and 7), recognize their extraordinary potential in the field of education, showcasing a well-rounded set of abilities.

5. Career Guidance: Gain insights into alternative career paths based on your child's date of birth,

allowing for informed decisions aligned with their unique numerological profile, beyond conventional professions.

6. Key Takeaways for the Chapter - How To Detect Education Sector?

1. Educational Potential: Use numerology to assess a child's education sector, unveiling insights into their academic capabilities, including the likelihood of excelling in studies.

2. Key Planets: Focus on the influence of planets associated with education and wisdom, particularly numbers 3 (Jupiter) and 7 (Ketu), as primary indicators of the child's date of birth.

3. Direct Presence: Emphasize the direct presence of numbers 3 and 7 in the date of birth for their significant impact on the education sector, distinguishing between the Driver, Conductor, and Kua numbers.

4. Exceptional Brilliance: Recognize exceptional brilliance in studies when both numbers 3 and 7 are present in the chart, predicting academic success and a reputable career for the child.

5. Aligning Career Expectations: Acknowledge the importance of aligning career expectations with a child's numerological profile, avoiding mismatched aspirations that may lead to dissatisfaction and lack of fulfillment.

7. Key Takeaways for the Chapter - Profession Of Anti & Opposite D-C Combination

1. Opposite Combination Professions: Avoid professions aligned with both Driver and Conductor numbers in opposite combinations (e.g., D=4, C=2). Opt for numbers present in the chart that are compatible with both Driver and Conductor, such as 3, 7, and 6 in the given example.

2. Anti-Combination Professions: Similarly, refrain from professions associated with both Driver and Conductor numbers in anti-combinations (e.g., D=1, C=8). Choose alternative numbers present in the chart that are comfortable with both Driver and Conductor, like 5 and 6 in the provided case.

3. Number Compatibility: Understand the compatibility of each number with the Driver and Conductor, selecting

professions based on harmony and synergy with these influential numbers.

4. Avoidance of Conflicting Professions: Prioritize avoiding professions directly associated with conflicting numbers in opposite or anti-combinations, ensuring alignment with the chart's overall dynamics.

5. Identifying Opportunities: Keep an eye out for opportunities that align with the chart's strengths, such as recognizing the silver lining in a chart with a complete line of 2-5-8, indicating potential success in real estate, property, and agriculture sectors.

8. Key Takeaways for the Chapter - Trying Hard To Get A Government Job?

1. Government Job Yogas: Explore the presence of yogas for government jobs in your date of birth, emphasizing the influence of numbers 8 and 5 in numerology.

2. Saturn's Role: Understand the significance of Saturn in numerology, being the planet responsible for government jobs, particularly associated with the number 8.

3. Numerical Complement: Recognize number 5 as the complement of number 8, also contributing to the likelihood of government job yogas.

4. Combined Influence: If both numbers 8 and 5 are present in your date of birth, it strongly indicates a favorable alignment for pursuing a government job.

5. Sector Suitability: Consider banking and finance as a suitable sector for individuals with numbers 8 and 5, given their financial associations and compatibility with government job yogas.

9. Key Takeaways for the Chapter - Who Can Be A Coach And A Player?

1. Career Roles Defined: Understand the role that suits you in your career—whether you excel as a player, coach, consultant, or teacher—based on the presence or absence of specific numbers in your date of birth.

2. Key Numerical Players: Identify the crucial role of numbers 5 and 6 in becoming a successful player and numbers 3 and 7 in excelling as a coach.

3. Inner Power Significance: Acknowledge the importance of numbers 5 and 6 in providing inner power and soul to your chart, enhancing your potential in the player's role.

4. All-Rounder Possibilities: Explore the possibility of being an all-rounder in both coaching and playing if your chart includes numbers 3, 5, 6, and 7.

5. Product vs. Service Numerology: Differentiate between suitable numbers for product-oriented careers (5 and 6) and service-oriented professions (3 and 7), guiding decisions on starting a factory, school, or brokerage service.

10. Key Takeaways for the Chapter - Mobile Numerology

1. Mobile Numerology Simplified: Demystify mobile numerology; it's not as complex as advertised. Learn to calculate the compatibility of the last ten digits in your mobile number with your driver, conductor, and overall chart.

2. Exclusion of Country Code: Disregard the country code when evaluating your mobile number. Focus solely on the last ten digits for numerological analysis.

3. Avoid Numbers 4 and 8: Steer clear of mobile numbers with a total sum resulting in 4 or 8, as these numbers are considered unfavorable in numerology.

4. Consider Digit Pairs: Assess the pairs forming the single-digit total, emphasizing the significance of the first pair. Avoid numbers where digits within a pair are incompatible.

5. Attention to First Digit: Ensure the first digit of your mobile number is not antagonistic to your driver and conductor. Avoid starting with 8 if your driver is 1, for example. Exclude numbers starting with zero, except in specific circumstances, and explore call forwarding for number transition.

11. Key Takeaways for the Chapter - Design Your Visiting/Business Card

1. Visiting Card Significance: Understand the importance of your visiting card; it's a key element in portraying

your honor and personality, influencing your professional success.

2. Premium Design Elements: Design business cards with a premium look to enhance their impact and reflect positively on your professional image.

3. Color Harmony: Emphasize correct color combinations on your business card. Align the color choices with your numerological chart for a harmonious and auspicious impact.

4. Strategic Information Placement: Ensure proper placement of crucial details like name, address, phone number, company name, and logo on the card. The diagram provides a visual guide for optimal positioning.

5. Symbolic Design Choices: Incorporate symbolic design elements, such as placing the logo in the middle for balance and featuring the company name in italic fonts to signify continuous and dynamic progress. Tailor color selections based on your numerological chart for added alignment.

12. Key Takeaways for the Chapter - Top-5 Case Studies

1. Authenticity of Date of Birth: Verify the accuracy of the client's date of birth, as discrepancies can lead to misinterpretations. Case Study 1 illustrates how a client's actual date, not the officially documented one, held the key to understanding life challenges.

2. External Influences on Success: Consider external factors impacting an individual's success. Case Study 2 demonstrates how a spouse's favorable chart can significantly contribute to the success of the other partner.

3. Center Number's Significance: Emphasize the importance of the center number in a chart. Case Study 3 highlights the challenges faced by an individual with missing center number 5, despite having an otherwise impressive chart.

4. Profession and Numerology: Connect the suitability of a profession with specific numbers. Case Study 4 reveals

how the absence of healing-related numbers led a doctor to switch to a successful career in law.

5. Name Spelling Impact: Investigate the impact of name spelling on an individual's life. Case Study 5 demonstrates how an incompatible name spelling acted as a source of marital issues despite a seemingly stable chart. Applying filters, including name spelling, can unveil hidden aspects affecting one's life.

IMPORTANT! - BEFORE YOU PROCEED

Important Note to Readers

Dear Readers,

Before embarking on the insightful journey presented in this book, "Master Your MONEY With Numerology," we highly recommend delving into the foundational knowledge provided in the first six chapters of the Numerology Mastery series – "Master Your DESTINY With Numerology." These initial chapters serve as the cornerstone for understanding the core principles and concepts that underpin the world of numerology.

In "Master Your DESTINY With Numerology," we unravel the mysteries of numerology, exploring the profound connections between your date of birth and the intricate tapestry of your life. The insights gained from these foundational chapters will lay a robust groundwork for comprehending the advanced concepts and applications discussed in this present volume.

Kindly Download Your "Free Book" Here By Scanning the QR Code Click the Link Below:

"FREE MASTERY BOOK"

The mastery of numerology is a progressive journey, much like building a house where a sturdy foundation ensures the strength and stability of the entire structure.

Likewise, the knowledge gained from the initial chapters acts as the bedrock, enhancing your ability to grasp the intricacies of financial empowerment explored in "Master Your MONEY With Numerology."

By familiarizing yourself with the foundational principles, you'll be better equipped to extract maximum value from the advanced techniques, personalized analyses, and strategic insights presented in subsequent chapters. We encourage you to absorb the wisdom shared in the earlier segments to fully harness the transformative potential that numerology offers on your path to financial mastery.

Thank you for your commitment to self-discovery and empowerment through numerology.

Wishing you an enriching and enlightening reading experience.

Warm regards,
Sooraj Achar
Author, Numerology Mastery Series

CHAPTER ONE

FIND YOUR SUITABLE PROFESSION - JOB OR BUSINESS?

"Align your professional journey with the cosmic rhythm of numbers to unlock unparalleled success in your career."

C an we predict whether a job or business will be a good fit for us by examining our date of birth (DOB)? Let's explore this in the following chapter. The answer depends on our driver, conductor, and chart.

1

Here are the best options for Driver numbers from 1 to 9:

1= Business

2= Job

3= Both are good

4= Business

5= Job is preferable but business is also good

6= Business

7= Job

8= Business

9= Business

If your driver and conductor form an opposing or contradictory combination, it's advisable not to base your choice of business or job solely on the driver or conductor. Instead, select a number that is harmonious with both your driver and conductor, ensuring it's also present in your chart.

Choosing a specific number for a job doesn't mean that individuals with that driver cannot excel in business. They can indeed thrive in business if they have favorable Yog and lines in their chart.

For instance, if your driver is 7, and conductor is not anti or opposite, and you have a complete line of 2-5-8 in your chart, then you can excel in business. More specifically, aligning with the complete line, you can excel in property and real estate business. Although 7 is associated with jobs, due to its connection with healing and the occult, it's recommended to explore job opportunities in these fields.

CHAPTER TWO

DETECT YOUR FOREIGN OPPORTUNITIES & ABROAD SETTLEMENT

"Discover the numerical blueprint of your professional destiny and sculpt a path that resonates with your true calling."

I n this chapter, we will learn which country is best for you:

- The Country in which you are born

- Or a Foreign Country

If you have choices, we can decide which country is best for you among your choices.

Numbers for foreign settlement are:

I) 6 - Venus

II) 5 - Mercury

- If number 6 is present in your chart, you should try your luck abroad.

- If number 6 is absent but 5 is present, you can try your luck abroad. But number 6 is more responsible for foreign settlements.

- Number 6 carries a 100% chance of success in a foreign country and number 5 carries 50%.

- In the chapter "Complementary Numbers", we discussed that the number 5 is complementary to the number 6 and the number 5 does not have any complement.

- If 5 and 6 are both present, it means if you cannot get settled abroad, no one can. You must go abroad and try your luck in a foreign land. Foreign land is far better than your birth land.

- If 5 and 6 are both absent, don't think about settling abroad. If you still settle, you have to struggle much more.

How can you select a specific country?

Let's understand with an example:

Suppose these are the countries you want to settle in.

First of all, let's find numerical values for all countries.

- **USA = 631 = 10 = 1**

- **CANADA = 315141 = 15 = 6**

- **UK = 62 = 8**

- **AUSTRALIA = 163421311 = 22 = 4**

- **NETHERLANDS = 55455231543 = 42 = 6**

After knowing the numerical value of a country, match your **driver number** with that numerical value. If it matches, you can settle in that country. If it is not, you cannot.

- If you are ruled by the number 8, you should not go to the USA. Canada and the Netherlands are good for you.

- If you are ruled by the number 3, you should not settle in Canada or the Netherlands because 3 and 6 are anti-numbers.

You can check for any country and find which country is good for you according to your driver and conductor number.

India or Abroad Settlement

Which country is good for us? Should we stay in our motherland or is it better for us to settle abroad? Let's look into dates of birth and find the answer with the help of numerology.

Numbers for Foreign Settlement:

- 6= Venus

- 5= Mercury

- 4= Rahu

If these numbers are there in your birth you can do much better in foreign. 6 is a very powerful indication for foreign success, 5 is slightly less powerful and 4 is considered as a weak indication. If 6 & 5 both are in your chart there may be a very huge success waiting for you abroad. If you don't have these numbers you can still settle abroad but your spouse should have either 6 or 5 or both in their chart.

Now let us understand further with some examples

Example 1:

Suppose a DOB is 06-05-1980. The birth chart is-

D= 6

C=2

This chart is a perfect example of foreign settlement because 6 and 5 both are present.

Example 2:

Suppose a DOB is 7-05-1982. Here is the chart-

D= 7

C=5

In this case, 6 is absent but 5 is present. And there is no contradiction between driver and conductor. This date of birth is also good for foreign settlement.

Example 3:

Suppose a DOB is 8-07-1972. The chart will look like this-

D= 8

C= 7

Because both 6 and 5 are absent, it is a clear-cut indication that this person should not consider foreign settlement. If he/she tries to settle abroad, he/she will have to face many problems and will ultimately end up staying in their motherland. In the event that their spouse has 6 or 5, they can consider trying to settle abroad.

Example 4:

Suppose a DOB is 12-07-1990. The chart is-

D= 3

C= 2

Because of the absence of 6 and 5 foreign settlements aren't good for this DOB. but this DOB is very good for staying in India. Because the total of INDIA is 3 (1+5+4+1+1= 12; 1+2= 3) which is the driver number of this DOB.

Selection of a Country:

If you have the option to choose from many countries, here is a method by which you can select a perfect country that suits your date of birth. First, you need to calculate the total of that country by adding the numerical value of the country's name. This value should be a single digit, so you need to keep adding the digits until you obtain a single-digit number. After obtaining this number, compare its compatibility with both your driver and conductor. This number should be compatible with both your driver and conductor. Now, you should select the country that is most suitable for both your driver and conductor.

Let's have a look at Canada first. The total of CANADA (315141) is 6.

Now let's look at Dubai. The total of DUBAI (46211) is 5.

The total of USA is 1. (6+3+1)

The total of UNITED STATES OF AMERICA is 5.

If your driver is 3, Canada may not be a suitable country for you. If your driver is 8, the USA is not a good option to settle. We are considering the USA over the United States of America because it is more common.

You can use the same formula if you're going to select a school or university. Just add the university's name to obtain a single-digit number and compare it with your driver and conductor.

CHAPTER THREE

PROFESSIONS AS PER THE LINES IN YOUR BIRTH CHART

*"In the symphony of your career, let
numerology be the guiding melody that leads
you to the pinnacle of success."*

I n this chapter, we will learn about the professions
attached to 8 lines or yogas in our birth chart.

Vertical lines

A. 4-3-8 = thought plane

Number 4 denotes knowledge, 3 denotes logic and 8 denotes dedication.

Politics works very well for this person and this plane is also called the plane of politics. If not political, the second best profession is marketing, then sales, then law and judiciary.

B. 9-5-1 = will plane

All professions are good for this plane. Because 9 and 1 are common in all persons born in the last century, so 9 and 5 have less significance therefore 1 plays a crucial role here. Specifically, the banking sector is the best choice for this type of person. They can also take a chance in agriculture, property, and real estate because number 5 is the most powerful number among earth elements.

C. 2-7-6 = action plane

These people are very good at physical exercise. They can build a huge career in sports like cricket, football, hockey, etc. They can also do very well in the business of luxury, fashion, and beauty. Because it has a pair of 2-7 they can do good in the fields of the occult (vastu, numerology, taro, astrology, etc).

Horizontal Lines

A. 4-9-2 = mental plane

These people have a very sharp mind and very strong memory. They can do well in mental sports like chess. They can do wonders in science and mathematics. The computer industry and software industry are also good options.

B. 3-5-7 = Emotional Plane

When 3 and 7 are there in your chart you can blindly jump into the professions of occult and healing. You can be a talented doctor or a good teacher. You can go into the education field and can open wellness centers. Administrative jobs are a very good option.

C. 8-1-6 = Practical Plane

These people can do very well in the commercial world. They are successful in business and entrepreneurship. They can choose any business of number 6 like the business of luxury and glamor, hotel industry, salon, etc. If you don't want to do business there are also opportunities in the law and judiciary sectors. These people can also try their luck in politics.

Diagonal lines

A. 4-5-6 = Raj Yoga 1

It's the most amazing line. These people can earn exponentially in the Hotel, restaurant, saloon, luxury, glamor, garment, casino liquor businesses, etc.

B, 2-5-8 = Raj Yoga 2

If you have this line you are born for real estate, property, and agriculture. If you can't do this you can invest in these sectors. On the other hand banking and financial sectors are a good choice because 5 and 8 are very strong here.

CHAPTER FOUR

FIND YOUR LUCKY & UNLUCKY COLORS

"Craft your professional narrative with the wisdom of numerology, turning challenges into stepping stones and goals into realities."

Friendly and Non-Friendly Colours

In this chapter, we will learn to decide which colors are friendly and which are non-friendly to us. And how we can use them in our lives.

You can see the color of a particular number in the table below.

Num	Planet	Colour
1	Sun	Red
2	Moon	White
3	Jupiter	Yellow
4	Rahu	Black & Gray
5	Mercury	Green
6	Venus	White
7	Ketu	Black & Gray
8	Saturn	Black
9	Mars	Red

Now we will take an example of my date of birth and will figure out which colour suits me.

Suppose my date of birth is 13-02-1967, and this is my chart.

4	9	22
3		7
	11	66

D=4 C=2 K=6

Whichever color you choose should match your driver and conductor.

And we can find this match in the chapter "Compatibility of numbers".

- Red can be my lucky number because red is the sun's color and the sun's number is 1 which is a friend of my driver (4) and conductor (2).

- White is also my lucky number. Because it is matching with my conductor.

- 3rd number yellow (the number of Jupiter) is also okay with my driver and conductor, so yellow can also be my lucky color.

- Black is not matching with my driver and conductor, so it is my non-friendly color.

Everyone should avoid black color until it does not match with your driver and conductor. Because black absorbs natural light, this is the color of darkness and who wants to live life in darkness? This is also the color of Rahu,

Ketu, and Saturn, which are struggling planets, so this is a color of struggle.

The Colour of the number 5 (color of Mercury) is green, it is the friend of everyone, so green is the friendly color of everyone.

Now you can pick each number and match it with your driver and conductor. That's how you can identify your friendly and non-friendly colors.

The Luckiest/Most Important Colour for you:

If the color is matching with your driver and conductor and this number is missing from your chart, it becomes the most important color for you. You must use this color.

Also, remember these points:

- In any condition, if your driver or conductor is 1, black is dangerous for you.

- If your conductor or driver is 4, 8, and 2, you must avoid black.

- If your driver or conductor is Jupiter's number

(3), you must avoid white.

- If your driver or conductor is 6, you should avoid yellow.

Colors may not be the deciding factor in your overall perspective.

Colors are not the deciding factor in your success. But colors can work as catalysts in the progress of our life. Colors can decrease or increase the progress of our life.

While we have the option to choose colors, why should we not use them according to our date of birth? There is no reason we should not use colors in our life.

- You can choose the color while purchasing a car.

- You can choose the color for your home.

- You can choose the color of your garments and undergarments.

There are many more examples like this.

Shades of colors will be considered as the main colors.

For example, you can consider pink as red when you are calculating your lucky color. If red is your lucky color, then pink is too.

Hope you found your favorable colors.

Colour Sharing Planets

There are some planets that share the same color. For example, the Moon and Venus have the same white color. Similarly, Rahu and Ketu have the same grey color, and the Sun and Mars have the same red color. This creates confusion when writing about lucky colors. In this chapter, we are going to eliminate this confusion. We will learn which number should take priority whenever there is a conflict.

These are the planets and their colors:

1. Sun- Red

2. Moon- White

3. Jupiter- Yellow

4. Rahu- Grey

5. Mercury- Green

6. Venus- White

7. Ketu- Grey

8. Saturn- Black

9. Mars- Red/Orange

First of all, let's discuss numbers 2 (Moon) and 6 (Venus), both of which share the color white. The Moon is a gentle, delicate, and somewhat slow planet, whereas Venus is aggressive, attentive, and brimming with luxury and glamour. When we compare the two, Venus is more powerful and dominant in terms of its traits. Due to Venus's greater strength, it has a larger influence on the color white compared to the Moon.

Now, let's consider numbers 1 and 9. The Sun and Mars both share the color red. There is no conflict regarding the color orange, as it is solely controlled by Mars. Because the Sun possesses more power, it has a greater influence on the color red in comparison to Mars. Therefore, number 1 will exert a stronger dominance over the color red.

Myth About Black Color:

There is a myth that if your Driver or Conductor is 8, you should wear black as much as possible because it is supporting your Driver or Conductor. This myth is completely wrong and illogical. Actually, if your Driver or Conductor is 8, you should never wear black, as it is the color of Saturn, which is a struggling planet. By wearing black, you are increasing your struggle. Instead, you should donate black items (such as clothes, sweets, pulses, etc.) as much as possible.

CHAPTER FIVE

IS YOUR CHILD
WEAK IN STUDIES?

*"Navigate the complexities of your career
with numerological insights, making strategic
decisions in harmony with your cosmic code."*

T here is a question in the mind of every parent about whether their child will study or not. In this chapter, we will be checking if your child has yogas of study and what is the level of that yoga. Every parent wants their child to be brilliant in studies. Every parent wants their child to become an engineer, a doctor, or IPS and IAS officer.

We will be talking about formal and informal education and what type of education is suitable for your child.

Write your date of birth and your driver and conductor number on paper. Do the same thing with the date of birth of your child. If number 3 and number 7 both are present in the date of birth of your child, he/she has an exceptional ability to study. 3 is the number of Jupiter and 7 is the number of Ketu. 3 is the number of knowledge and 7 is the number of wisdom. If someone has both knowledge and wisdom, he can do extremely well in the field of education.

After checking both numbers 3 and 7, check if the top line (line of 4,9,2) of the Loshu grid is supporting or not.

If your child has all five numbers, it means he/she is an extraordinary child.

Now let's talk about other combinations:

If your child has only one number, either 3 or 7. He/she can still do well in studies. But remember, number three is the primary number of education. If your child has neither 3 nor 7. It doesn't mean that your child cannot do well in their studies. But informal education is suitable for him/her.

In a hypothetical situation, suppose your child has 5 and 6 in his/her date of birth. Your child can go into media, hotel management, tour and travel, and the fashion/glamor industry instead of becoming a doctor, engineer, or officer.

Chapter Six

How to Detect Education Sector?

"Uncover the hidden energies within your professional aspirations and harness them for enduring success and fulfillment."

In this chapter, we will determine the Education sector of a child according to his/her DOB. We can predict if the child will be good in studies or not in the education field, whether will he study or not, and how far he will study.

The planets associated with education and wisdom govern this sector. When examining the education sector, our primary focus should be on numbers 3 (associated with Jupiter) and 7 (associated with Ketu). It's important that these numbers are directly present in the date of birth. If they stem from the Driver or the Conductor numbers, their influence is less potent. Moreover, if these numbers are related to the Kua number, they will have no significant impact on this sector.

Let's understand with the help of some examples:

Example 1:

Suppose the DOB of a male child is 14-03-1997 and the chart is-

D= 5

C= 7

K=3

Because 3 and 7 both are present in the chart this child will be exceptionally brilliant in his studies. He will be doing very well in his school and college and will get a very reputable job.

Example 2:

Suppose a dob is 15-04-2010, he is a male, and here is the chart-

D= 6

C= 4

K=8

As you can see this chart has Raj Yoga of 4-5-6 and 8-5-2 but both 3 and 7 are absent. We are doing wrong with this child if we are forcing him to study to become an IAS, Doctor, Engineer, etc. This DOB is the DOB of an entrepreneur, this is the DOB of a businessman. This person is going to build his own empire. This child should be given informal education, he can graduate and can do any course related to business of his interest. We should not expect an Engineer or Doctor from this child. I am not saying that he can not become an engineer or doctor but he will be unsatisfied in that position, he will feel suffocated in that field, and he will try to escape from that profession because he is not made for these professions.

MAY I ASK YOU FOR A SMALL FAVOR?

I want to express my sincere gratitude for choosing to invest your time in reading this book. Your decision to explore this work among countless others means a lot to me.

I hope that within these pages, you've discovered actionable insights that can enhance your daily life. Your journey doesn't have to end here, though.

May I kindly request an additional 30 seconds of your valuable time?

Sharing your thoughts about the book through a review would be immensely appreciated. Your review serves as a beacon, guiding other readers to take a chance on my books. It's a small gesture that carries significant weight in the world of authors.

To submit your review effortlessly, please **Scan** the **QR Code** below. It will take you directly to the book's review page:

"Master Your PROFESSIONAL GOALS With Numerology"

Alternatively, you can also find the "**Reviews Section**" of this book's page on Amazon.

Your review will require just a minute of your time but will make a monumental difference in helping me connect with a broader audience and I eagerly look forward to reading your review.

Once again, thank you for your unwavering support of my work.

CHAPTER SEVEN

PROFESSION OF ANTI & OPPOSITE D-C COMBINATION

"Numbers aren't just symbols; they are keys
that unlock the doors to a fulfilling and
prosperous professional life."

I n this chapter, we are going to learn about the detection of profession for anti and opposite D-C combinations.

Professions for Opposite combination:

For example, let's take a DOB of the opposite D-C combination- 13-02-1967. Here is the birth chart:

D= 4

C=2

K=6

We should choose a profession that suits our Driver as well as Conductor. But in this case, the profession of number 4 (driver) is not suitable for the profession of number 2 (conductor) because both are opposite numbers.

In the cases of opposite combinations, we should avoid the professions of both driver and conductor. Instead, we can go for the professions of any other number present in our chart but that number should be compatible with our driver and conductor both.

Let us understand further with the example above, these are the numbers present in that chart:

4: Must avoid its professions because it is 'anti' to our conductor.

9 & 1: It is my advice to all persons born in the last century to ignore numbers 9 & 1 because these numbers are common in all of them.

2: number 2 is not suitable with the driver and the conductor therefore we will avoid it.

3: numbers of Jupiter and neutral with driver(4) and friendly with conductor(2). We can choose the professions of the number 3.

7: this is the number of Ketu which is highly compatible with driver and conductor. We must go with this number.

6: this is the number of Venus which is also highly compatible with driver and conductor therefore we can go with the professions of number six in this case.

Professions for Anti combination:

The process of selecting professions for 'anti' combinations is exactly the same as the process of 'opposite' combinations.

Suppose a DOB is 10-05-2000, the driver is 1 and the conductor is 8, it is an anti-combination. Here is the chart:

D= 1

C= 8

K= 9

Because driver and conductor are opposite to each other we must avoid the professions of number 1 and 8.

Now we will look for the professions of other numbers present in the chart:

8: It is anti to our driver so we must avoid it.

1: It is anti to our conductor so we must avoid it.

5: It is comfortable with both driver and conductor therefore we can go with the professions of number 5.

9: This is the KUA number in this case and KUA numbers are weak numbers so we should avoid them.

Silver Lining: because the line of 2-5-8 is complete in this chart this is an amazing chart. Real Estate property and agriculture are the best sectors for this chart. Money will rain from these three sectors for this particular chart.

While looking at the chart we should keep looking for these types of opportunities so that we can extract the best of the best from the Date of Birth.

This is how we can choose the professions of opposite and anti-D-C combinations. Now it is your exercise to make some charts of opposite and anti combinations and find the best profession according to their chart.

CHAPTER EIGHT

TRYING HARD TO GET A GOVERNMENT JOB?

"Numerology isn't just about numbers; it's about understanding the language of success written in the stars of your professional journey."

E veryone wants a government job and people always ask me whether they will get a government job or not. Do you have Yogas of government job in your date of birth? Let's discuss this in this chapter.

There are two important things, first the government job and second, the sector in which we are going for the service.

Is this the banking or railway sector that is suitable for you? Or your date of birth is suitable for the income tax department?

Let's figure this out.

According to numerology, Saturn is the planet that is responsible for government jobs. So we can say that government jobs are given by number 8.

Write your date of birth and driver conductor numbers on paper.

If number 8 is present in your date of birth, you have very strong yogas for government jobs.

Number 5, which is the number of Mercury and the complement of number 8. This is also responsible for government jobs.

If you have number eight, definitely you can think of a government job. If you don't have the number eight, you can look at the number 5.

If you have both numbers, you must go for a government job.

The suitable sector for the person with numbers 8 and 5 is banking and finance.

Number eight is called a financial number because it is the number of Saturn.

The same thing is applicable to number 5 because it is the complement of number 8.

Chapter Nine

WHO CAN BE A COACH AND A PLAYER?

"Aspire, achieve, and ascend in your career
by decoding the numerical secrets that shape
your professional identity."

B ased on one's date of birth (DOB), we can predict whether providing services or selling products is a better fit. In any job or business, you can either sell products or provide services. In this chapter, we will explore whether you can excel as a coach or as a player, can you be a good consultant or you are a great teacher, depending on your DOB.

Sachin Tendulkar is an amazing player, but can he also be a good coach? Maybe, or maybe not. His coach was a very accomplished mentor who developed a player like Sachin Tendulkar, but didn't he ever consider that if he could train a player like Sachin, he might have been an even better player than Sachin?

Salman Khan is a very good actor but behind him is his director. But Salman Khan cannot be a director and his director cannot be an actor like Salman.

So we need to understand the role that suits us. We need to understand what role is made of me and in what role I can do best.

Let's understand with some examples:

If you have 5 and 6 in your chart your chart is wonderful even though you don't have a complete line. If you have each number present in your chart but 5 and 6 aren't there your chart doesn't have soul, your chart does not have the inner power, your chart is that factor. Therefore you can understand how important these two numbers are.

- If number six is present in your chart you can be a good player.

- If numbers six and 5 both present in your chart you can be a very good player.

- If only 5 are present you can be a good player.

- If 5 and 6 both are absent you can be a good coach.

- If 5 and 6 are absent but 3 is present you can be a good coach.

- If 5 and 6 are absent but 3 and 7 are present, it's an indication of becoming a very good coach.

- If only 7 are present you can be a good coach.

- If you have 3, 6, and 7 you can be a good coach while being a good player at the same time. You can be an all-rounder in this case.

- If 5, 6, 3, 7 all four numbers are present then it is the most beautiful chart. The person can be a very good coach and a very good player at the same time. He is the best of all-rounders.

"In short, numbers for becoming a player are 5 and 6 and numbers for becoming a coach are 3 and 7."

"For services, numbers 3 and 7 are most important and for products numbers 5 and 6 are important."

If someone wants to start a factory it means numbers 5 and 6 are important for him because he is going to sell products. If someone wants to start a School, numbers 3 and 7 play a role here because he is now going to provide services. If you want to trade in the stock market then number 5 and 6 are important because you are doing like a player. But if you want to start a brokerage service then 3 and 7 should be there in your DOB because brokerage is a consultancy business.

This was all about this chapter I hope you understood.

CHAPTER TEN

MOBILE NUMEROLOGY

*"Your professional goals are written
in the language of numbers; embrace
numerology to translate them into tangible
accomplishments."*

There are so many advertisements circulating about mobile numerology. They are showing that it is a very hard thing to learn but believe me it's not rocket science. Let's learn this in this chapter.

We don't need to account for the country code when choosing our mobile number. Consider a mobile number like +91 9818073751; in this number, +91 is the country code for India. Since it's the same for every number issued in India, and because it is common to every phone number, it doesn't affect the numerology. Therefore, we only need to calculate the last ten digits of our mobile number. The total of these ten digits (until it becomes a single-digit number) should be compatible with your driver and conductor. For example, the total of the above-mentioned number is 49 (9+8+1+8+0+7+3+7+5+1), which is further reduced to 13 (4+9). After adding 1 and 3 together, we get a single-digit number, '4'. This single-digit total represents our mobile number, and all principles should be applied according to this number.

Checklist for selecting a mobile number:

1. The end total should be highly compatible with the driver, conductor, and chart.

2. Don't consider country code and city code while calculating the end total.

3. Avoid number 4. Suppose a mobile number is +91 9818073751. The total of all ten digits (we

are not considering country code) is 4. Four is the number of Rahu and it should be avoided. If your mobile number has 4 as its total you should avoid buying that number even though it is compatible with your driver and conductor.

4. We should also avoid 8.

5. We also need to check the pairs from which our single-digit end total is coming. In example one our first two-digit number was 49. Numbers 4 and 9 are not compatible with each other so we should avoid this type of number.

Suppose another mobile number is 9818073750, after adding all digits of this number we will get 48, four and eight are opposite of each other so we should avoid this number.

(only the first pair is most significant)

1. The first digit of the mobile number should not be Anti to your driver and conductor. If your driver is one your number should not start with 8.

2. There should not be zeros in your mobile number. You should avoid zeros. But if the end total is very good and the starting number is also compatible then one or two zeros are acceptable. If there are more than three zeros then you must avoid that number.

3. If you have a very old number that is not according to your DOB and you cannot easily change that number, in that case, you use the call forwarding option. Buy a new compatible number and forward all calls and messages from the old number to the new number.

CHAPTER ELEVEN

DESIGN YOUR VISITING/BUSINESS CARD

"Numbers are the architects of destiny; let them design a blueprint of success for your professional endeavors."

I n this chapter, we will learn to design business or visiting cards. Your visiting card is important for your success. Your visiting card describes your honor and your personality.

- Business cards should look premium.

- Use correct color combinations.

- The company name and your name should be in the correct place.

You can see the correct positions of name, address, phone number, company name, and logo in the diagram below.

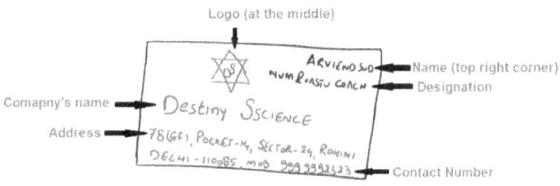

Points to Remember:

- The logo should be in the middle of the card.

- The company's name should be in italic fonts. The italic font style represents running and continuity. So your company always keeps running.

Select color combinations according to your chart.

CHAPTER TWELVE

TOP-5 CASE STUDIES

"Master the art of blending ambition with cosmic alignment, as numerology guides you towards the zenith of your professional goals."

I n this chapter, I will share with you some special cases I faced as a numerologist.

Case Study-1

This client was a male. His date of birth was 22-10-1968. You can see his chart below:

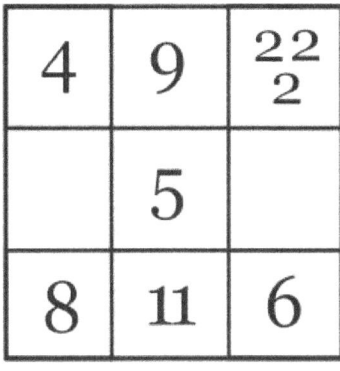

D=4 C=2 K=5

After looking at his chart, I said to him, "Sir, your date of birth is amazing. Both the diagonals of your chart and the yogas of 951 are complete. You must be enjoying your life."

But his answer was very surprising. He replied that for the last 30 years; he had been doing a normal clerk's job and he only owned a scooter. He was not in the condition of purchasing a car.

After having this fantastic chart, how is it possible that he was living an ordinary life? Definitely, there is something hidden we are not able to see.

Then I asked him, "Are you 100% sure this is your date of birth?"

He replied, "This date of birth is written on my PAN Card, Aadhar Card, and on all other official documents, but that's not my actual date of birth."

Then I asked him about his actual date of birth, and he told me that 26-06-1967 was his actual date of birth.

I again made a chart according to his actual date of birth:

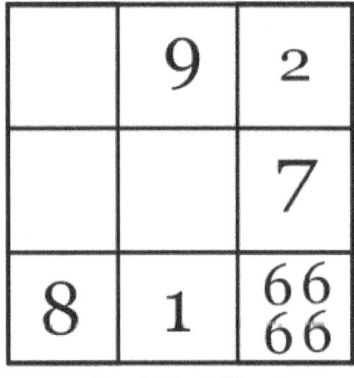

D=8 C=1 K=6

Actually, his driver number was 1, and the conductor was 8. It's one of the worst combinations. He also had four times 6 in his chart, which is a complete symbol of disappointment. Also, number 5 was absent from his chart.

The reason behind the disappointment in his life was his actual date of birth.

The idea is- if you have to face this type of issue, you can cross-question your client if he is confirmed by his date of birth or not. If a client's lifestyle does not match their date of birth, maybe they are telling you the wrong date of birth.

<u>Case Study-2</u>

This client was also a male and his date of birth and chart are as follows:

DOB: 07-03-1978

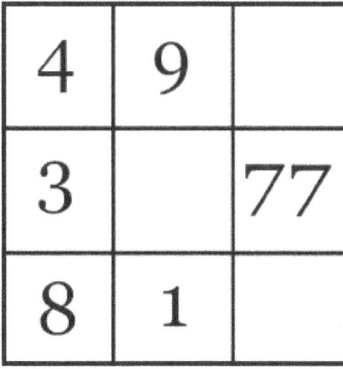

D=7 C=8 K=4

When he showed me his date of birth, I told him "You haven't achieved much in life. Your married life is also looking disturbed. You have abilities, but you are not able to grab the maximum output from your abilities and you haven't built your house yet."

You will be surprised by his reply. He replied, "It's been 15 years since I got married and I am living a very happy married life. It was a love marriage and there are no issues in my marriage. Everything is going well in my life and I own two houses. I also have a good bank balance."

I was amazed because his words were not matching with his date of birth. Then a thought came into my mind and I asked him about his wife's date of birth.

His wife's date of birth was 15 07 1982, then I made a chart of his wife:

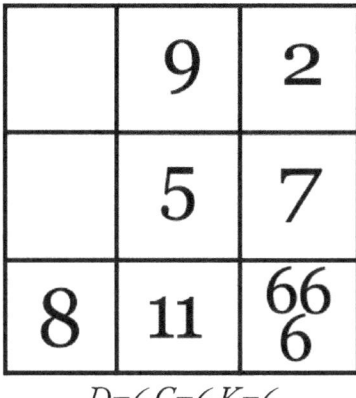

D=6 C=6 K=6

When I observed his wife's chat, I asked him a question- "when did you get everything, before your marriage or after your marriage? It looks like you got all these things after your marriage."

He replied- "yes you are right! I became successful after my marriage,"

Now you know the reason for his success. You can see in his wife's chart that her driver-conductor combination is very good. There is Venus in the first place and Venus in the second as well. This combination comes in the top 10 combinations among all 81. Also, the yoga/line of 9,5,1 is complete in her chart.

His wife was the reason for his ultimate success.

You have to face these types of problems and you have to use mind applications to solve them. You have to cross-question your client to know the correct reason behind the success or failure of the client. Sometimes things are more complicated than usual, but everything is according to what you read in numerology.

Case Study-3

This client was also a male. His date of birth and chart are as follows:

DOB: 24-08-1987

44	9	2
3		7
88	1	6

D=6 C=3 K=4

At first glance, this chart looks very awesome. 8 out of 9 numbers are present, and four lines are complete, but the only problem in the chart is that the center is absent. Because the center is absent, this person might be facing many ups and downs in his life. And the most important thing is that his driver is 6, and the conductor is 3. Which is one of the worst combinations.

I asked him a question: "Are your business and life stable?"

He replied, "No!"

And when I asked about his marriage, he replied that he had gotten divorced.

This example teaches us the importance of the number 5 in the chart. After having eight numbers and four complete lines, he was still struggling in his life; he had everything but nothing.

If someone's chart looks beautiful, if someone has almost all the numbers present and many complete lines, there are still chances that they are not successful.

<u>Case Study-4</u>

This client was female and her date of birth and chart were as follows:

DOB- 26-05-1964

4	9	2
	5	
8	1	666

D=8 C=6 K=6

Doesn't it look like a fantastic date of birth? Her driver-conductor combination is good; both diagonals are complete and one vertical line/Yoga (951) is also complete.

I told her- "your date of birth is amazing, you have everything in your life with a little bit of struggle."

She replied- "Yes! I have almost everything, a good car, a good house, and a good bank balance."

Then she added- "I am a doctor (gynecologist) but I left medicine as a profession 30 years ago, and now I am running a law firm."

What is the learning session in this case?

She had everything, but number 3 and number 7 were missing. Both numbers are most important to be successful in the healing profession and she didn't have both. She had number 8 in her chart, that's why she was successful in the law sector. Also, number 6 was present, which is a supporting planet for the law sector.

She shared some more information. She told me that she got divorced in her first marriage and now she is in her second marriage.

You cannot predict multiple marriages after looking at her chart. Then I asked her about the date of birth of her ex-husband. Her ex-husband's date of birth was 11-11-1960 his driver number was 2 and her driver number was 8. How can it be a stable marriage when the combination of drivers is not good?

Case Study-5

This client was a female and her date of birth and chart are as follows:

DOB: 22-02-1968

4	9	22 2
	5	
8	11	6

D=4 C=2 K=5

She was facing problems in her married life. She told me that her marriage failed twice. But in her chart, the stability of marriage is looking good. The driver number is 6, and the conductor is 9, so there may be some minor issues, but that's all normal. Then what was the actual problem?

To know the actual reason behind it, we need to apply some filters.

The first filter I applied was name spelling. When I asked her about her name spelling, her name's spelling was number 3. Which is an anti-number to her driver (6).

Her name spelling was the main reason behind all the issues.

So whenever you face a problem like this, first of all, try applying a name-spelling filter. Sometimes you have to apply many filters to know the exact reason, but 80-90% of the time, people have problems with their name spelling.

CONCLUSION

Congratulations on reaching the culmination of this book. Your commitment to reading through these pages signifies your dedication to personal growth and a thirst for knowledge. Completing a book is a remarkable achievement, and you should take a moment to acknowledge your accomplishment.

Throughout this journey, the aim has been to guide you toward shaping a destiny defined by success and fulfillment. Your investment in this book reflects a deep commitment to self-improvement, and for that, you should feel proud.

As you conclude this book, I trust that it has left you with valuable insights and a sense of empowerment. The road to a prosperous destiny is not always linear or without its challenges, but your newfound knowledge in smart questioning equips you to navigate these paths with confidence.

I genuinely hope that your voyage through these chapters has been both enlightening and engaging. The pursuit of a splendid life brimming with happiness and fulfillment is a commendable one, and your proactive steps toward this aspiration are evident through your persistence in reading this book.

In the pursuit of success and a life well-lived, remember that knowledge is your most potent tool. With this, you hold the key to unlocking the limitless potential within you.

As you close this final page and embark on the journey that follows, I extend my heartfelt best wishes for a future filled with accomplishments and contentment.

Cheers,
Sooraj Achar

MAY I ASK YOU FOR A SMALL FAVOR?

I want to express my sincere gratitude for choosing to invest your time in reading this book. Your decision to explore this work among countless others means a lot to me.

I hope that within these pages, you've discovered actionable insights that can enhance your daily life. Your journey doesn't have to end here, though.

May I kindly request an additional 30 seconds of your valuable time?

Sharing your thoughts about the book through a review would be immensely appreciated. Your review serves as a beacon, guiding other readers to take a chance on my books. It's a small gesture that carries significant weight in the world of authors.

To submit your review effortlessly, please **Scan** the **QR Code** below. It will take you directly to the book's review page:

"Master Your PROFESSIONAL GOALS With Numerology"

Alternatively, you can also find the "**Reviews Section**" of this book's page on Amazon.

Your review will require just a minute of your time but will make a monumental difference in helping me connect with a broader audience and I eagerly look forward to reading your review.

Once again, thank you for your unwavering support of my work.

PREVIEW OF MY BEST SELLING BOOKS

1. Numerology Mastery Series

★ **Why do 80% of People Fail to Recognize their True Potential ??**

These self-help books will help you **Recognize, Transform, and Navigate** your life toward a **Happier Destiny**.

I always say that your **Date of Birth** is so precious. God has placed many diamonds on your date of birth that you are not aware of. It doesn't matter if your date of birth is good or bad. The idea is how you can take the best out of your date of birth. **Master Your DESTINY With Numerology** is a perfect, **complete beginner's guide** for those who are new to numerology.

★ What Role Does Numerology Play in Your Life?

- You have been surrounded by numbers since the day you were Born. Now use them to unlock your Destiny.

- Wherever you go in your life, the numbers always move on with you.

- When you are born, on the very first day of your life, you get your date of birth, which is made up of numbers.

- When you get admitted to school, you get your roll number.

- When you get your results, you get a percentage of numbers.

- When you get a job, you get a salary and EMP-ID number.

- When you buy any vehicle, it has a number plate.

- When you travel, you get a ticket and seat number

- When you check into a hotel, you get a room number.

- When you want to call a person, you have to dial numbers.

- When you get married, there is also a date attached to it.

- If there is Life, there are Numbers. You cannot get rid of Numbers.

★ Your **Name Spelling** also plays an important role according to your date of birth. Believe me or not, **30% to 40%** of your success or failure depends on your name spelling. If you keep your name spelling correct, you can achieve 30% to 40% more success in your life.

♥ Master Your DESTINY With Numerology will help you...

✓ Recognize Your Strengths and Weaknesses.

✓ Find Your Lucky Numbers and Colors.

✓ Correct Your Name Spelling without changing your documents.

✓ Choose the Right Profession.

✓ Find a Compatible Life-Partner.

✓ With Simple Remedies for All Your Problems.

✓ Check Your Foreign or Abroad Opportunities.

✓ Predict your Future Years, Months, and Days of importance, which helps you make Better Decisions.

✓ Understand the Behavioral Patterns of People Around You.

✓ Transform and Navigate your life for a Better Future.

★ If you are ready to make a commitment to yourself that you want to learn everything that is presented to you, then it is our commitment to you that this will surely help you a lot. There is no reason why this book will not change your destiny or transform your future. But, there is an important thing you must keep in mind, i.e., **"You will bring this change through TRANSFORMATION, not through MIRACLES".**

★ If you learn **Numerology**, then

(a) "You will be **awakened**", which makes it likely to " **transform**" your life.

(b) Ultimately, "You will be able to **navigate** your life".

★ Life is all about "**Awakening**,", "**Transformation**," and eventually, "Knowing How To **Navigate** It?"

★ Order **Master Your DESTINY With Numerology** now to make the most of your **Health, Relationships, Career, and Money** by unlocking the **Power of Numbers**.

Check Out Numerology Mastery Series Books Here

 **1. Master Your DESTINY With Numerology**

 **2. Master Your NAME-SPELLING With Numerology**

 **3. Master Your RELATIONSHIPS With Numerology**

 **4. Master Your MONEY With Numerology**

 # 5. Master Your PROFESSIONAL GOALS With Numerology

2. Vastu Mastery Series

★ **How Can These Books Work Miracles in Your Life?**

This Self-Help Book is A Perfect Blueprint Describing Ancient Principles for Modern Living. A Step-by-step Practical Guide for Beginners to Creating a Positive Living Space and for Optimal Well-Being.

Learn:

★ **How to Implement Feng-Shui/Vastu in your Day-to-Day Life !!**

★ **What Role Do Feng-Shui and Vastu Play in Your Life?**

★ Relationship between Vastu and Feng-Shui?

Vastu is used to Diagnose, and Feng Shui is the Remedy. Vastu is used to identify the disease, and Feng Shui is the medicine. Vastu and Feng Shui are complementary to each other.

Vastu Shastra is an Ancient Indian Science of architecture and construction, which is based on the principles of harmony and balance between humans and their environment. The main focus of Vastu is to create a harmonious balance between the 5-Elements of nature, i.e., Earth, Water, Air, Fire, & Space. It emphasizes directions and orientation and uses various elements like colors, shapes, and materials to create a balance and positive energy in the living spaces.

Feng Shui, on the other hand, is a Chinese Philosophical System of harmonizing everyone with the surrounding environment. It is based on the principles of Qi (Chi), the life force that flows through all living things, and Yin and Yang, the balance of opposite forces. Feng Shui focuses on the placement of objects, furniture, and structures in living spaces to optimize the flow of energy, or "Qi." It also considers the orientation of the building, the placement of doors and windows, and the use of colors, shapes, & materials to create balance & harmony.

In summary, both Vastu and Feng Shui aim to create balance and harmony in living spaces, but Vastu is more focused on directions and orientation, while Feng Shui emphasizes the flow of energy & balance of opposing forces.

★ **The Benefits of Reading This Book Include:**

✔ **Health and Well-Being:** Vastu principles aim to create a harmonious and balanced environment that can promote physical, mental, and emotional well-being.

✔ **Financial Prosperity:** Vastu principles are believed to help attract positive energy and good fortune, leading to financial prosperity.

✔ **Improved Relationships:** Vastu principles can help create an atmosphere of peace and harmony, which can lead to improved relationships with family, friends, & colleagues.

✔ **Increased Productivity:** A Vastu-compliant environment is said to be conducive to productivity and efficiency, leading to greater success in personal & professional life.

✓ **Spiritual Growth:** Vastu principles are based on ancient Vedic knowledge and aim to promote spiritual growth & enlightenment.

✓ **Enhanced Creativity:** Vastu principles are believed to enhance creativity and inspiration, which can be beneficial for artists, writers, & other creative professionals.

✓ **Better Sleep Quality:** Vastu principles can help create a peaceful and relaxing environment, which can improve the quality of sleep and help reduce stress & anxiety.

✓ **Improved Mental Clarity:** A Vastu-compliant environment is said to help clear the mind and improve mental clarity, which can be beneficial for decision-making & problem-solving.

✓ **Enhanced Career Prospects:** Vastu principles can help align one's career goals with their personal strengths and abilities, leading to greater career success & satisfaction.

★ Overall, the benefits of Vastu can contribute to a more Balanced, Harmonious, & Fulfilling Life.

★ Order "Master Your DESTINY With Vastu" now to make the most of your Health, Relationships, Career, & Money by unlocking the Power of Directions.

Check Out Vastu Mastery Series Books Here

 ## 1. Master Your DESTINY With Vastu

 ## 2. Master Your GROWTH With Vastu

3. Master Your WEALTH With Vastu

4. Master Your CAREER With Vastu

3. The Ultimate Self-Healing Mastery Series

"The Art of Balancing Yin-Yang Energy" is an enlightening and transformative guide that unveils the ancient wisdom of harmonizing the opposing forces of Yin and Yang within ourselves and the world around us. Drawing from the profound teachings of Eastern philosophy and modern-day practices, this book offers a comprehensive understanding of Yin and Yang and provides practical techniques to achieve balance, harmony, and fulfillment in all aspects of life.

In today's fast-paced and chaotic world, finding balance is more crucial than ever. Whether you seek to improve your relationships, enhance your well-being, or achieve success in your career, understanding and aligning the Yin-Yang energy within you can be a game-changer. This book takes you on a transformative journey, guiding you through the principles, practices, and benefits of embracing the art of balancing Yin-Yang energy.

By delving into the core concepts of Yin and Yang, you will gain insights into their dynamic interplay and learn how to identify and rectify imbalances in your life. Discover how the complementary forces of Yin and Yang manifest in various aspects, such as work-life balance, emotional well-being, and personal growth. With this knowledge, you can cultivate harmony and create a fulfilling and purpose-driven life.

★ Here are the <u>Top-15 Benefits</u>:

1. Harmony and Balance: Balancing yin-yang energy promotes a sense of harmony and balance within oneself and in relationships with others.

2. Enhanced Well-being: Balanced yin-yang energy contributes to overall physical, mental, and emotional well-being.

3. Stress Reduction: Maintaining balanced yin-yang energy helps reduce stress and promotes a state of calmness and relaxation.

4. Increased Energy: Balancing yin-yang energy enhances vitality and boosts energy levels.

5. Emotional Stability: Harmonizing yin-yang energy supports emotional stability, reducing mood swings and promoting emotional resilience.

6. Improved Focus and Clarity: Balanced yin-yang energy enhances mental clarity, concentration, and focus.

7. Better Decision-Making: When yin-yang energy is in equilibrium, it fosters better decision-making skills and promotes sound judgment.

8. Enhanced Intuition: Balancing yin-yang energy can amplify intuition and inner wisdom.

9. Improved Relationships: Harmonizing yin-yang energy cultivates healthier and more balanced relationships, promoting understanding and cooperation.

10. Greater Creativity: Balanced yin-yang energy can enhance creativity and innovation in various aspects of life.

11. Physical Healing: Balancing yin-yang energy supports the body's natural healing abilities and can contribute to faster recovery from illnesses or injuries.

12. Emotional Healing: Harmonizing yin-yang energy aids in emotional healing and facilitates the release of emotional blockages.

13. Enhanced Digestion: Balanced yin-yang energy promotes optimal digestion and helps alleviate digestive issues.

14. Hormonal Balance: Balancing yin-yang energy can help regulate hormonal imbalances and improve overall hormonal health.

15. Improved Sleep Quality: Harmonized yin-yang energy promotes better sleep quality and can help alleviate sleep disorders.

Check Out Self-Healing Mastery Series Books Here

 **1. The Art of Balancing YIN-YANG Energy**

 **2. The 7 Energy Needs**

 **3. The Fear of Death**

4. The Purpose of Your LIFE

5. The Power Of ONE Question

TESTIMONIALS

These are a few feedbacks from my clients across different parts of the world. Kindly go through their reviews to understand how Numerology and Vastu helped them.

1. Ekta Gupta – Kolkata, India

"2021 is a difficult year for me. I have consulted a few numerologists. I have received vague answers and complicated solutions. I'm new to numerology. Charges were expensive. Sooraj is a good and kind soul. He is very patient with me. He answered all my questions. I had 1000 questions. More ever he helped me to find a business name with no extra charges. I'm grateful to him. With your

help, I'm sorted out with my business name. I had a lot of anxiety about it. I'm confident now. Sooraj is a helpful soul. He is patient and explains if one has questions. He doesn't rush into closing the job. You can consult him easily. I am going to recommend him to newbies like me. He is not going to cheat you or misguide you".

2. Neetu Ganglani - Stanley, Hongkong

"Hello Sooraj, I can't thank you enough. At the age of 45, I could find an ideal life partner for myself. And my compatibility with the boy I like. Got to know our strengths and weaknesses. Your suggestions helped me to find the right life partner. You have a bright future. Good luck"

3. R Lensly Kwaimani - Solomon Islands, Oceania

"Dear friend, glad I came across you. My daughter Felinda Kwaimani is sick for a long

time and I was very much worried. Thank you for giving suggestions and guidance".

4. Seham Shabhir - Talagang, Pakistan

"You're one of the best numerologists...your predictions are correct...you are a very humble person...you gave answers to all of my questions in detail ... I'm very thankful to you. Ur remedies prove very helpful for me. He is the very best numerologist... I recommend him for all.. u should consult him to get rid of your problems..his remedies work like a magic"

5. Naveen Kumar - Bengaluru, India

"Sooraj is a gem as a human and as a professional. Before approaching Sooraj, I have enquired and got inputs from other numerologists and I did some research as well. I Was not satisfied with the answers provided by them and most of them were behind fees,

even after paying for the consultation they charge extra for clarifying doubts. However, Sooraj was awesome in client satisfaction and the way he follows up with the client for providing suggestions. He takes the initiative to follow up and provide the best solutions and describes the reason for the input. I definitely suggest Sooraj to anyone who is looking for start-up business names or anything related to numerology. He has a good amount of knowledge and patience to answer all my queries".

6. Sneha S - Karnataka, India

"Hi Sooraj, it's a great prediction starting from Personality Traits to our Abroad Opportunities to future achievements. Everything is perfectly predicted with correct proof and explanations which help us to understand our lives better and take steps accordingly to numerology. Everyone are

curious to know more about their life just to know when, how & what situations they will come across and how they need to overcome everything. Thanks a lot, Sooraj, for the best Numerology Prediction which helped us to understand ourselves better".

7. Aditya S - Mumbai, India

"Sooraj, your numerology predictions are brilliant and accurate. Your Suggestions helped me find out whether my current job is suitable for me or not. I would suggest people consult you in due course of time".

8. M Nabanita - West Bengal, India

"Hi Sooraj, it's helpful and gives me a quick idea and help. Thank you so much for being there. It helped me to understand my situation It helps in my career and marriage. The information is good".

9. Naresh Kumar – Bangalore, India

"Hello Sooraj, it was satisfactory. Can decide further based on the info shared & also can see positive outcomes looking forward to checking how it works".

10. Harishchandra Dnyaneshwar Deshmukh – Delhi, India

"Hi sir, Padhai puri nahi kar paya, 11 k salary he, Stable nahi hu life me, Business success nahi milta. Thank u sir for sharing my report and helping me understand my strengths and weaknesses".

AUTHOR PROFILE

 Follow **Author's Profile Page** to get updates on all his books: **https://amazon.com/author/sooraj_achar**

 Grab your **Free Gift** if you missed it: **https://gift.sooraj-achar.com/**

Please Leave Your **Valuable Review** here: **Master Your PROFESSIONAL GOALS With Vastu**

For 1-to-1 consultation, scan the **QR code** or contact: **connect@sooraj-achar.com**

Follow the **Author's BookBub** Profile: **BookBub Author Profile**

Stay Connected to the **Author's Social Media Handles** below:

https://amzn.to/3CgQHF9

https://medium.com/@soorajachar99

https://bit.ly/3M7gIu2

instagram.com/psychology_of_numberz/

https://bit.ly/3dO6aDh

https://bit.ly/3LXBTyz

https://bit.ly/3E9vKxc

DISCLAIMER

This book is for educational purposes only. Readers acknowledge that the author does not render legal, financial, medical, or professional advice. The content within this book has been derived from various sources. Please consult a licensed professional before attempting any techniques outlined in this book.

By reading this document, the reader agrees that under no circumstances is the author responsible for any direct or indirect losses incurred as a result of the use of the information contained within this document, including but not limited to errors, omissions, or inaccuracies.

Adherence to all applicable laws and regulations, including international, federal, state, and local governing professional licensing, business practices, advertising, and all other jurisdictions, is the sole responsibility of the purchaser or reader.

Neither the author nor the publisher assumes any responsibility or liability whatsoever on behalf of the purchaser or reader of these materials. Any perceived slight of any individual or organization is purely unintentional.